Hannah Chutzpah is a performance p⸍ ss.
Born and raised in London ⸍s
performed everywhere (
Albert Hall. Her one-wc
received five star reviews
a good way.

Hannah has been described ⸍iree therapists, as
'of good character' by a high ⸍ judge and as 'a potential
maggot-thrower' by the Metropolitan Police.

This is her third collection.

Permeable

Hannah Chutzpah

Burning Eye

Burning Eye Books
Never Knowingly
Mainstream

This edition published by Burning Eye Books 2017

www.burningeye.co.uk
@burningeyebooks

Burning Eye Books
15 West Hill, Portishead, BS20 6LG

ISBN 978-1-911570-03-5

Dedicated to my Mom & Pop,
who raised me to Give A Damn
and try just about anything creative.

Thank you.
(Sorry about the swearing.)

CONTENTS

PHYSIOLOGICAL

SAFETY

LOVE AND BELONGING

ESTEEM

SELF-TRANSCENDENCE
AND SELF-ACTUALISATION

The sections of this collection follow Maslow's Hierarchy of Needs:

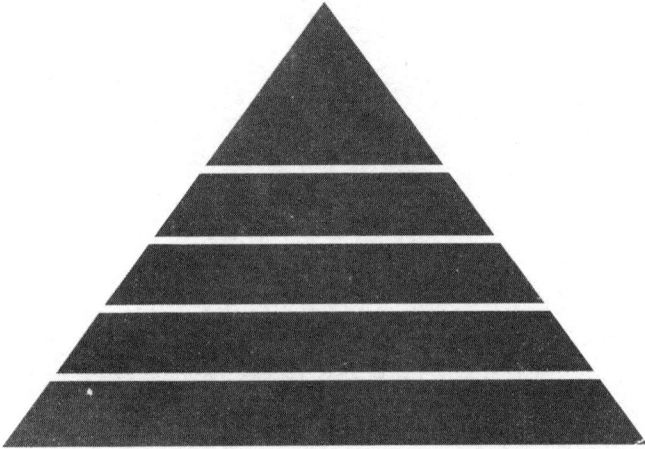

From top to bottom, the levels of the pyramid are:

Self-transcendence & self-actualisation
Esteem
Love & belonging
Safety
Physiological

Abraham Maslow (1908–1970) was an American psychologist who proposed the Hierarchy of Needs in his 1943 paper 'A Theory of Human Motivation'. The theory states that we need to cover our basic and survival needs before we can move on to 'higher' goals

It's much disputed and criticised now, but it is definitely true that when your basics are sorted you are much freer to think further and achieve more.

'Millennials' have been raised with a lot of insecurity around the basics of jobs and housing. It doesn't always stop us, but it often erodes us.

PHYSIOLOGICAL

HUG

When I hug
My hands are gentle fists
Against the other's back
Scared of opening palms, fingers pressing
Scared of intruding – too familiar, too close
Even as my own back sinks into their
Open palms
Pressing welcome
Into my grateful skin.

THIS IS YOUR TWENTIES

This is your twenties:
Thank God for Facebook, emails and mobile phones
Because if we were landlines and Filofaxes
Everything would be scribbled out three times –
'Til we switched to pencil for everyone.
Each page crumpling under the weight of its history:
Each erased address a ghost of a houseshare.
Forwarding addresses and forgotten postcodes.

This is your twenties:
Postcodes make good additions to passwords.
A techie taught you that
Seven jobs ago.

This is your twenties:
The impermanence isn't painful per se
But it takes something from you
This lack of solid ground.

This is your twenties:
And you are one of the urban nomads
Lives organised by smartphones
And scuppered by batteries or broken screens.

This is your twenties:
And 'Goodness, you've got a… diverse CV.
Can you talk it through with me?'
Listen, hundredth recruiter, if it looks scrappy
It's because there are just scraps of jobs going.

This is your twenties:
How did you lose so many nights?
How did you gain so many lighters?
A detritus gathering that you need to get clean of
– and you will –
Just as soon as you find the time.

This is your twenties:
You're in the prime of your life
But you've now had more jobs than sexual partners
And you think you might be doing this wrong.

This is your twenties:
Music and memories are digitised or discarded
Because who has room for hard copies?

This is your twenties:
And you're sure that dead laptop
Had something important on it
But it's moving time again
So keep or throw?

This is your twenties:
Your years of experience are growing into something harder:
Not quite armour
But people seem to think you're equipped now.

This is your twenties:
Crises typed for broadcast in the small hours
Agonies answered with animal GIFS
Because our loved ones are always reachable
But usually too far away
To give us a hug.

This is your twenties:
Every object aching with memories
And each one a burden as you box and unbox
Moving from postcode to postcode
And pick where to plant your roots
This season.

This is your twenties:
And every next step could be The One
Where you find the job with the pension scheme
You'll actually use
Or the person you'll grow old with

But each maybe is scattered across your CV
Each pension contribution cooking in pots
Too small to keep track of
Each nearly-there relationship reminding you how close
– and yet how far –
You are
From ever finding

Home.

SAFETY SCISSORS

Masking tape marks the boundary
Yellowed cream on brown carpet
I decorated it with felt-tip
Badly.
This line draws the battle lines:
This line you will not cross
This line I will defend with fists and feet
Claws and teeth.

Your bit is bigger.
The rest of the room
– demilitarised, Lego-strewn –
Is larger still.
I've left you all that.
I'm being the reasonable one
And if you step over my line
I will kill you.

When we fight: I don't feel the blows.
My only thought, every time
Is frustration
That I do not have the strength
To inflict the damage I want.

If I were strong enough:
I would tear out hair and scalp
Bite out chunks of flesh
I would hobble you, humble you.
If I were strong enough
You'd finally see:
I am one to be feared.

But my only thought, every time
Is frustration.
I am plastic safety scissors
When I want to be a sword.
I am plastic safety scissors when I want to be a sword.
I am plastic safety scissors when I want to be a sword.

I need to be
I need to be
I need to be a sword.

If I were loud enough:
I would shout you down.
Tantrum, tick or TV
If you talked over me:
I would shriek sonic boom
'Til you whimpered and ran.

If I were bold enough:
I wouldn't care
About their disapproval
That I am the normal one
That I should know better.
An ounce less self-respect
And I could match you.
I would yell and hit and get away with it
Like you do.
It's only fair.
Anyway, you're older.

If I were powerful enough:
I would have high walls built
Of solid granite.
Nothing less than a system
Of space-age airlocks
And medieval drawbridges
To decide who can come in
And who is kept out.

But masking tape marks the boundary
Yellowed cream on brown carpet
I decorated it with felt-tip
Badly.
This line draws the battle lines:

This line you will not cross
This line I will defend with fists and feet
Claws and teeth.

The cat's allowed in.
I like her.
Anyway, she's a girl.
No boys allowed.

WILDERNESS

Old enough to know that hugging
Is for babies and girls
He refuses
Drifts, untouched, for years
Dreaming of a girl
To kiss and hug.

TUMBLEWEED

They said we could be
Tall as redwoods
Bright as autumn maples
Bold as monkey puzzles
But to survive
We are learning to be tumbleweeds.

In another life
I would dig weeds
Plant trees
Learn every flower's name
Watch the seasons' green pulse
Across my landscape.

But we know we never stay
Long enough to see
The fruits of our labour
So our gardens grow
Neglected:
Brambles, fag butts, plastic bags.

We uproot after each season:
Each tenancy
Each fixed-term contract.

Each time a phone is lost
We scatter new numbers like grass seed
Hope the lawn will grow back
As lush as before.

In another life
We could be ecosystems
But here we ache to evolve
Fast enough
To adapt to each environment:
New neighbourhoods
New neighbours' names
Register again for doctors, dentists, votes
We have grown callouses

Where others grow roots
We are stunted
Bonsai.

They said we could be
Tall as redwoods
Bright as autumn maples
Bold as monkey puzzles
But to survive
We are learning to be tumbleweeds.

JOB CENTRE

Surviving the job centre
With your ego intact
Is a masterclass in
Unsolidarity.

Wear the office clothes
You no longer have to.
Wear the smile of someone
Momentarily inconvenienced.
Like your career got a flat tyre
And this is the garage.

When the security guard escorts you
From desk to desk
(Same as everyone)
Treat them like a valet service:
Thank them with an indulgent smile.

Have a book with you
A large one
With a sombre cover.
Carry a nice pen in your pocket.
Sail through the patronising print-out forms
With the air of a business-class traveller
Checking in.

Do not turn your head to the screams
Of children in prams.
Do not look worried when
A claimant shouts and slurs
Two seats away.
Act as if everyone else is behind glass.
Pretend you are not permeable.

Do not let it flicker across your face
That rent is looming
That you are too bored to be well
And too broke to go out

That this is the first time you have worn shoes
In three days
That your days consist of forgetting meals
And remembering biscuits
While the mess stacks around you.

You are wearing nice shoes now.
The ones you bought
Before redundancies were announced.
Delicately correct typos and grammar
In the photocopied forms
Like a supervisor.
Like *their* supervisor.

Under ugly ceilings
The fluorescent strip-lights
Glint off your armour
Of accent, degree, CV.

You are not one of them
Honestly

You are just visiting.

BLOOD BONE BOWEL BRAIN BREAST

At the cancer charity temp job
I update the website with this year's stats:
Incidence, recurrence, survival rates
At one year, five years, ten years.

Every task is a body part
Every to-do list is a surrealist poem
Today it reads:
Blood
Bone
Bowel
Brain
Breast

Most pages grow a person's name:
Blood: that kid my brother knew growing up (he didn't)
Bone: a family friend (five years ago)
Bowel: an old teacher (according to rumours)
Brain: my grandmother (before I was born)
Breast: my old colleague (I should send a card)

Sometimes I'm reaching:
Pancreas: Bill Hicks

My computer password is Fa1rySara
A nod to my godmother.
I think of her every time I type it in
Mean to call her
More often than I do.

The graphics are bright and clear
Talk of fundraising and improving survival rates.
I have read the house style guide.

I have ordered and memorised
The top five most deadly cancers.
I have diagnosed myself with four.

But even from down in the trenches
Typing all the raw, miserable numbers
I still snicker when my manager says:
'Skip brains for now, work on skin'
Or
'Testicles after lunch, please.'
I still want a prize for not shouting
'WA-HEEEEEY!'
When she tells me
'It's breasts and alcohol today.'

I think Sara would find it funny too
But since a page has grown her name
I don't tell her.

CASE STUDY

Mel – not her real name –
Studied English at a good university.
She never wanted to be a journalist
Because of the questions she'd have to ask.

'Did your kids ever see him hit you?'
'Why would the police do that to your brother?'
'Tell me about your first Christmas on the streets.'

But this is her job.
The trauma must be just right for harvest:
Not too raw, not overripe or therapist-stale
Spoken in clinical terms of abuse, misuse, and issues
Which need translating back to their full horror

For the annual review
The commissioners' report
The fundraising email.

Mel – not her real name –
Draws out each person's life, releases it by consent form
Packages its best and worst parts in pithy pull-quotes
With a photograph where possible.
Faces incongruously happy
Now that We Have Helped.

She couldn't do this as a journalist.
But now she works for charities
The process is the same.

'How did you feel when you got the diagnosis?'
'What was the worst thing about the sex work?'
'Did you try to stop drinking on your own?'

Everyone understands it is For the Cause
To Raise Awareness
To Access More Funding
To Help Other People Like You

So they tell her their life stories
Methadone, rough sleeping, wife-beating and all
And she worries what her face is doing
Or what the correct amount of empathy is
When she's wearing her work clothes.

The people have discussed it with their keyworkers
They're glad to help the charity
They think Mel is a big shot
Because she came from head office.

The people aren't sure about using their real names
They might have to check with their parole officers
About photographs.

Mel – not her real name – always tries to end on a positive note
To tap a soundbite
That might become the headline
She asks questions which will demonstrate their progress.

'Can you tell me about your new home?'
'What's it like having your kids back?'
'How's the college course going?'

She assures them that they'll see a copy
Have a chance to change anything they like
Before it goes to print.

She is usually glad to do the job well
But says she sometimes feels
'Like a thief, or a misguided tourist'
And wonders if the annual review is enough
To justify this invasion.

FAIRY RINGS

Gentrification is a game
We have to play
But cannot win.
We move in mushroom fairy rings:

The unsafe neighbourhood   becomes
The OK neighbourhood   becomes
The cool neighbourhood   becomes
Unaffordable.

We spores settle where we can
Move when we're starved out.
We know we change each place
But we cannot change the pattern.

We have to play
But cannot win.
We move in mushroom fairy rings.

NON-NATIVE SPEAKER

I was never the most tactile person
Learnt touch like a second language
Too late to be fluent.

I can do confident, conversational
Confirmed relationships, handshakes and hugs
But as a non-native speaker
I still feel smart when I understand
Something complicated.

I flirt by weaving words
Leave a bubble of space
It is the other's option to breach, to burst
Or leave alone
As they wish.

You learnt touch like a mother tongue
Never scrimp on adjectives, arms interlocked.
Where I am unsure, you conjugate perfectly
Just the right nuance of contact, warmth
Confident in your movements
With me.

I feel smart when I understand
Something complicated
But here I am a touch hesitant
To ask for a translation.

LESS AIRBRUSH, MORE SEX

I am sat cross-legged in front of my mirror
Pulling faces
Trying and failing to chase the smirk
From the corners of my mouth.

Usually a mirror is an audit of situations.
Hair: tangled? Fluffy? Roots?
Skin: circles? Sunburn? Pores?
Teeth: spinach?
Weight: don't even.

But today I am seeing the things
He sees in me.
Today, I try to clamp down on that smirk
But I always end up grinning
Then giggling
Then gurning.
I have not enjoyed my reflection with this
Childlike, giddy glee, since the last time I was –

This morning, we woke to each other
Examined every eyelash and laughter line
In dozy, post-kiss zoom lens.
I couldn't believe how gorgeous:
The sharp contrast of brow and skin and stubble.
His muscles, I said, as I ran my hand over them
Were like salmon.
(Wrong simile. He's vegan.)

He told me my eyes are always mischievous
That just a look at my lips does things to him that…
And we giggled
And kissed
And swore we were leaving soon
And didn't.

I am sat cross-legged in front of my mirror
Looking at the things he sees in me:
Not assessments of imperfections but
Mischievous eyes
Red-hot lips.

I have not enjoyed my own reflection
With this childlike, giddy glee
Since the last time I was smitten
Seeing the things she saw in me
When I looked at a scar and saw gorgeous
Because it was her new favourite place
To plant a kiss.

Mirrors are more often
The first meeting of the morning.
Check the stocks and stats from overnight:
Hair: needs a wash
Skin: keep an eye on that spot
Teeth: lay off the coffee.

But today
I am sat cross-legged in front of my mirror
Pulling faces
Trying and failing to chase the smirk
From my red-hot lips.

SAFETY

FIRST AGAINST THE WALL

Once we used to take pride in
'We'd be first against the wall.'
Once the possibility seemed as distant
As being burnt at the stake.

Once we were envious of the heroes:
Right time
Right place
Right on
But now our time and place are wrong
We see clearly
Wish the fight weren't ours.

These days, some days
We can feel the targets being painted on our backs
Feel the brush clammy, the sickly chill, sticking clothes to skin.
Some days, it seems likely
That someone might decide
Our actions, thoughts, religion, skin, sex, love, location
Make us targets.

Now danger glints
In too many of our facets
We see our bravado was built
On shadowboxing.

May we stay safe.
May we remain uncompromised.

We still do what we used to – mostly.
We still say what we used to – mostly.
But the throwaway line has grown layers
Of target practice paint
'Til it is no empty brag but an admission:
We can't hope to scrub all the danger off
Live lives small enough that nobody could ever possibly –

We might be first against the wall.
It's no badge of honour, nor a defiant cry.
It's a heavy-hearted weighing up and a sigh:
'Might as well be shot for a sheep as for a lamb.'

SHITHEAD BINGO

'This is so shit, you can tell a woman designed it.'
Cross!
'That is SO GAY.'
Cross!
'I'm not being racist, right, but—'
Cross!

Shithead Bingo:
A game for hostile work environments.

Step one:
Create your Shithead Bingo card.
Select your targets
From stereotypes and disadvantaged groups:

- The elderly
- Sex workers
- Ethnic minorities
- Fat people
- Thin people
- People on benefits
- Women with small tits
- Female drivers
- Child abuse survivors

This is your Shithead Bingo card.

Create this card *in your head.*
You don't want a note lying around
That looks like the Brixton Bomber's
To-do list.

Pick nine squares each week for the starter game
Or twenty-five if you're playing Pro.
You are now ready to play Shithead Bingo.

Whenever a square on your card is called
By your shitty colleagues' shitty jokes:
Cross it off!

The bitter smile this gives you
Will distract you from digging nails into palms
Doodling violent doom
Or going to the bathroom – again –
To text a friend, self-harm or cry.

'She's just being a spastic.'
Cross!
'He never gets a round in. Fuckin' Jew.'
Cross!
'These are my tranny shoes.'
Cross!

If one week you find
Every square crossed off
Congratulations!
You have just won at Shithead Bingo!
Throw your arms in the air and shout
'FULL HOUSE!
FUCK YOU ALL!'

Defenestrate your computer
Along with any colleagues you wish.
Leave in a victory parade
Of security guards or police.

'Why don't we just send them all back?'
Cross!
'This week is totally schizo.'
Cross!
'Thick people shouldn't breed.'
Cross!

If you have been playing for weeks
And have not yet won
Remember you are not

Wasting years of your life
Surrounded by arseholes.

You are just playing a very long game
Of Shithead Bingo.

'This stapler is retarded.'
Cross!
'Don't touch that, you might get AIDS.'
Cross!
'I got so tanned this one time, I looked like a terrorist.'
Cross!

Be strong.
You know something they don't know:
Their punchlines are the bingo balls
Spinning in their cage
Predictable in their horror
Helping you to while away the day.

Don't get cross, just cross them off!
Two fat chick jokes – 88!

If your manager
(The one with the rape jokes)
Reviews your performance poorly
Brings up your bad attitude
And tells you to consider this a warning
Remember that he has crossed a line:
His shithead comments crossed off a whole line
By Wednesday.

Play the game.
Promise him you'll do better.
And you will:
Next week you'll pick a card so good
That by Friday
You'll be sitting in the job centre
Victorious.

BEACON

An abuser is a heat-seeking missile.
Why you?
Because you burn bright
And warm.

They were drawn to your beacon
As are moths.
As are friends.

Resist the temptation
To see your signs of life
As signs of weakness.
Do not view the world as they do.

Though you still feel the threat of it
Remember:
Very few will view
Your light
Through crosshairs.

Do not camouflage or draw shades;
Walk tall and proud.
Illuminate your own path
Spilling light like water
As soft wings flutter
To be near you.

TOO GOOD TO BE TRUE

Nothing tastes as good
As too good to be true.
The feast laid on so soon, so thoughtful
The warning signs flapping in the wind
Bright as bunting

Platters of praise you never knew you were hungry for
Everything enchanting
Elaborately concocted
And the way they smile while they watch you eat.

Nothing tastes as good
As too good to be true.
Sure, you've heard fairytale warnings
That offers this sweet are often false
But that happens to fools;
This is your happy ending.

Even after the reveal, the run
The scrubland scramble to safety
Friends' questions clawing like branches
The double-guessing, the doubt
Resolving to keep on
The long, slow trudge to return
New dishes never taste quite as exciting
As that feast
Where the warning signs flapped in the wind
Bright as bunting.

BLUE

At the traffic light an officer crosses
In front of us.
I look and list aloud:
'Bodycam, cuffs, CS spray, Taser.'

My mother sighs at the steering wheel.
Stares at me with an expression
Waiting
For me to be nice.

'You know, they're not all evil,' she says.

But I can't unlearn
The lessons learnt
After the click of the cell door lock
I can't stop clocking the details:

Sky blue bibs: 'friendly' intelligence gathering.
Camera crews: unfriendly.
Boiler suits: riot cops and ultraviolence.
Zip ties on belts: mass arrests.
Different letters on shoulder numbers: it's coordinated.
No numbers: run.

These days I scan for signs
Read the situation
The same way she taught me to read roads
Avoid alleys and unsafe streets.

But here we disagree:
She still sees civilians
Where I see soldiers.

VERDICT

After fighting you every inch of the way
They will commend your bravery.

When mud has failed to stick
They will praise your dignity.

If, despite their best efforts, you are still standing
They will pay tribute to your determination.

Their crisp suits –
Their slick soundbites –
Their magnanimous smiles –
Do not betray for a moment
That *they* fought you.
That *they* lost.

History will record your heroics
In their words:

Brave
Dignified
Determined

And you are
But that is less than half
                              the story.

DICKHEAD

I mention 'Dickhead'
And he asks me to narrow it down.
I explain I avoid saying her name
She is Dickhead and Dickhead is her
But for clarity's sake

I say her name.

I'm so out of the habit
That her syllables feel foreign object
In my mouth
Don't taste like I expect them to
I was braced for hot or sour
But this has no flavour
Sits inert, like a stone.

As my tongue prods at it
He is all apologies for digging up that distress
But the hurt has rotted away
Left something hard
Flavourless and unfamiliar.

Though I still walk the long way to avoid it
Time has turned my memories
More monument than crime scene
And this limp I got used to
Is lately more muscle memory
Than hurt.

I spit out the name like a fingernail
Tell him not to worry
Walk away, working on my stride.

LIPMELT

It is sweet, sweet, lipmelt soft
It is years of warm maybe
Of hidden smiles now arrived
As awkward-nervous to see me
As I am it.

It is sweet, sweet, lipmelt soft
Grown gradually, in afterglow
A trail of small kindnesses
Still warm from the road
It is feeling no fear at his height or strength
His fingers running through my hair
As he grips – holds – our lips less than an inch apart
It is that small gasp, expectant surrender
And then

It is sweet, sweet, lipmelt soft.

LOVE AND BELONGING

KISS

As music kisses ears
As grass kisses bare feet
As flame kisses Rizla
Sun kisses shoulders and necks
And bottles kiss lips

We don't.

MAE WEST

Cut!
Let's rewind
To before I read your flirting
As a sure-fire thing
Approached with all the nuanced subtlety
Of Mae West
Falling down the stairs.

Let's pretend I was bare-faced
Had not worn that dress specially
Let's pretend your flashbulb praise
Wasn't intoxicating.
Let's pretend I knew the difference
Between a pep-talk
And a proposal.

Cut!
Let's clapperboard back
To before that unscripted not-lovers scene
Let's pretend I'd kept that Mae West bravado
Holstered:
Just pleased to see you.

TETRIS (AS A RELATIONSHIP ANALOGY)

3…
2…
1…
GO!

In the early days it was easy.
We slotted together so perfectly.
For my every quirk
You had the reverse
Like an enzyme – a key to fit every lock
And together we broke everything down.
We erased every block on that screen
And we were free
Just you and me.

We made space for each other.
Friends? Who needs 'em?
Jobs? Fuck that.
Food? Maybe later.

All we needed was each other.
And those falling blocks seemed gifted from the heavens.
We were on a never-ending winning streak
Riding the wave of good fortune
Perfect fit after perfect fit
And we laughed, wide-eyed,
That we were getting away with murder
Couldn't believe how many last-minute changes
We could make work.

We had lazy days, on autopilot,
Where everything just went to plan.
We didn't even have a plan
But our **S**s and **Z**s stacked to the left and right
In neat little piles
Os tessellated into Lego brick walls
Then melted away.

We were entranced together
And even when you weren't there
Those blocks swam before my eyes
While that tune hummed around and around.

And I've heard you can actually win at this game
That with a high enough score a rocket appears
And you fly off into happily ever after
And I don't know if that's true or not
I've only heard rumours and fairytales
But I just know if I ever could win –
It would be this game.
With you.

But then we hit pause
– just for a minute –
Some real-life stuff got in the way.
When we came back, nothing was the same
Our winning streak was gone
It started with one little gap:
I'd said **L.**
You could've matched my **L.**
You act soppier than me and you're leaving a two-block gap here.
Would it really kill you to say you **L** me too?

And it wasn't great, but we'd fix it later
But that later never came.
We stacked our tetrominoes around it, higher and higher
But the gaps grew with every layer.
Seriously, what were you thinking putting that **T** there?
Or leaving your *Top Gear* magazines and socks all over my floor?
You were all **S**s and **Z**s misaligned
And I was waiting for the **I**
I'd lost where **I** fit in
Seriously, where the hell is that **I**? It could fix everything.

But now our screen is filling up too fast
And the last-minute changes no longer work.
We don't get away with murder anymore.
We don't get away with anything.
'What's that face supposed to mean?'
'No, I'm not being over-sensitive; you're being an arse.'

But now the world is piling in on us
And there isn't time to turn around
Because we're moving too fast to fix
There isn't even room to roll your Is
Because it's moving in split seconds
Faster and faster until

We have no moves left.
As the final tetrominoes entomb our screen
We both see –
For you and me, it's:

GAME OVER

We had a good run.

NO LITTLE WORDS

She glances at her watch.
Shit, is that the time?
She says, 'I'll have to love you and leave you.'
She holds my gaze a beat too long
Kisses my cheek
Slings her bag and leaves.

Not that I'm counting, but that's the third one this week.

And if I'm not imagining it
We've been playing this game for a while:
Picking up that one word
And testing the weight
Of its one open vowel:
Comfortable in the palm of the hand
Nearly on the tongue.

She calls me 'luvvie' a lot lately.
I upped the ante with 'moi luvurr'
(West Country accent added
To prove I'm joking?)

We each feel the word's weight
As we each watch the other's eyes
Searching for an answer to that unspoken question:
If I wasn't kidding –
If this was for real –
If I threw this word to you –
Would you catch it –
Or would you flinch?

We each feel the moments where it *should* be.
Moments as taut as a drum skin
Where anything that lands
Will resonate.
But it doesn't land:
It circles above
Present in our pauses.

My heart looped the loop, then howled
The day she told me she loved me
– in that top.
So, just so she knows:
I love this pub
I love this song
And our mate Joe: I love that guy.

But for now she'll love me and leave me
And when she teases me
(God, I love it when she teases me)
I'll 'love you, too'
Sarcastically.

And we'll watch each other's eyes
As we test its weight:
Heavy as marble
Delicate as an eggshell.

We are both calculating
And we are both cowards.

IN TENTS

In crowd
In-jokes
In fields
In the sun
In our element
      In tents.

In queues
In stalls
In fashion
Insolvent
In aftersun
      In tents.

In flip-flops
In wellies
Inelegant
In mud
Indefinitely
      In tents.

Insomnia
Inadvertent
Insult
In tears
Intervene
      In tents.

In grass
In smoke
Ingenious!
In heaps
In giggles
      In tents.

In bottles
Intoxicated
Incapable
In trouble
In hand
      In tents.

In the morning
Indisposed
Inevitably
Insufficient
In Rizlas
      In tents.

Introductions
Indescribable
Intriguing
Individuals
Into you
      In tents.

In glances
Indiscreet
Insatiable
In love
Indecent
      In tents.

In hugs
In hysterics
In our prime
Incandescent
In celebration
      In tents.

In photos
In memories
In my dreams
In goofy hats
In Arcadia
      In tents.

A DUDE IN AN EAST LONDON PUB HAS JUST OUT-JEWED ME

For Tim Wells

Judaism is an in-joke to me
A semi-secret identity
A smile when you find another
From your tribe.
'Oh, you were at that gig too?'
'Oh, you're a veggie too?'
'Oh, you're Jewish too?'

Yiddish is a breadcrumb trail I sprinkle
Into conversation
To see if anyone picks it up.

I am a half-Jewish, bisexual dual-national.
I live on a few fault lines
But I can blend right in
Or reveal my hand slightly
See if anyone picks up my clues:
Like more direct eye contact
Or gazing at another girl's lips.

Yiddish is my verbal garnish:
Adds so much texture
Couldn't cook a whole meal with it.

I leave breadcrumb trails
But tonight – four pints in –
I have drowned my subtlety.
Tonight I dropped a whole loaf of *challah* on the table:
'I liked your *frum* puns. I am Hannah Chutzpah.'

He shakes my hand
Replies in *three whole sentences* of Yiddish.
And a dude in an East London pub
Has just out-Jewed me
Just by speaking the language
I took my name from.

Helen Goldberg, Hinda Nisnievich
You would laugh if you could see me now
Your own great-granddaughter
Scrawling 'greenhorn' across her signature
In the Yiddish she cannot speak.

I dye my *shiksa* blonde hair darker
Am nostalgic for a New York I never knew
And wish for more links to the past
That you couldn't wait to escape.

Growing up second generation
Means growing grafted.
I flower in London soil.
The seam is small, the transplant took long ago
But the name I am happiest in
Is one I made up
Like you did at Ellis Island
Like my mother did in London.
Our tradition is transformation
…That, and shouting.

But I am a *shikkered shiksa* tonight
And a dude in an East London pub
Has just out-Jewed me
Just by speaking the language I do not speak
The language people use
To tell their kids to behave
To buy milk
To *kvetch*, to quip, to shout
In syntax, structure and sentences
In a language
– a whole language –
That I do not understand.

And my breadcrumbs are just breadcrumbs
A verbal garnish:
Adds so much texture
Couldn't cook a whole meal with it.

INSUFFICIENT

The licence to call your friend
All names under the sun
Expired.
Auto-renew failed.
Insufficient funds
In your joint account.

I CALLED YOU CAPTAIN

The good times we shared
Were worth weathering some storms for
So I cling on in my crow's nest
Spying for when the view will clear
But we've been adrift for months
And our goodwill supplies are running low.

I had more stashed, so I restocked on the sly:
Fresh water, rum, biscuits and bog roll
But we're still going to run out
And you still consume like there is no lack
You still drink like you don't care
If we are left with only saltwater.

I wait
For the circumstances
Which were your excuses
To bleed out
To float belly-up
To be dead and done.
I harpooned them one by one
So we could steer back
To clear waters, balmy winds
Back to when you were kind.

The tongue-lashings were funny once
But they've been growing crueller.
Lately they are all whip and no wit.

I have become book-keeper
Logging the long list of small slights
Of favours given and never returned
And I see if we do break apart
We will never break even
Because you have a lifeboat
You have no need to settle this debt
I will float on flotsam
You won't even get wet.

I scrub the decks, scrub pots and pans
Will kick myself later, for taking it lying down
But at the time it's just my most recent attempt
To mend our sails.
At the time I never know
That this is the last straw
The same way your keys are always in the last place you look
Only because
That's when you stop looking.

In the thin, grey light of day
I start to spy the end of our journey
Cold and clear as the dawn:
You just don't care.
You'd let this ship drift anywhere.
I have been skeleton crew for us both.
You won't lift a finger to steer this.
I am weary, weepy, wondering why
I ever called you captain.

PRIMARK

I have nothing to wear.
It's the day before your funeral
And I am in Primark
Looking for something pink or sparkly
Buying too many butterfly hairclips
Because I can't summarise you in one

And I don't know why I am apparently trying
To summarise you in hairclips.

It's the day before your funeral
And I am titting about
In fucking Primark
With fucking hairclips.

It's stupid and it's frivolous

And I know you'd understand.

REPLIES RARELY

SexyCat31 replies rarely.
Non-smoker.
Thirty-two.
Sagittarius.
Doesn't have pets.
Wants kids.
Is an atheist but doesn't take it too seriously.
The most private thing she's willing to admit is:
'Lol not telling!'
Her family deleted her Facebook, LinkedIn, Twitter
But her OkCupid lives on.

Cocktails and cleavage profile pictures
Aren't often the ones families choose
For the memorial service.

Unseen messages pile up
Untouched
Deadmail
Turned her 'friendliness' rating from green
(Replies frequently)
To amber
(Replies selectively)
To red.

SexyCat31 replies rarely.
Her pixels now starlight:
Reaching you after the source has expired.

NECROKITTY COMIC SANS

I have good news and bad news.
The good news is that there is an afterlife
And pets get there too.
The bad news is that in that afterlife
There is really mawkish poetry.

Dear pet crematorium
Thank you for returning my cat's ashes
Along with a candle and a white flower
(That was a nice touch).
However, I do have some questions
About the poetry.

Dear pet crematorium
Could you please talk me through
The four poems you gave me
Three apparently written by my dead cat
Two of them addressing me as 'mum'.

Dear pet crematorium
I am no one's mum.
I've had some wild nights in my time
But I do not recall ever
Giving birth to a cat.

Dear pet crematorium
I never knew my cat could speak English.
If I'd known she understood me
I would have called her nicer things
Than Munchkin, Fuzzbutt, and Bastardface.

Dear pet crematorium
Why was she holding out on me all this time?
And are you sure these are from her?
Only I think her scansion would be better.

Dear pet crematorium
It hurts that she chose to communicate
From beyond the grave

In Comic Sans.

Dear pet crematorium
Why is my dead cat writing
To tell me to be strong?
She knows I'm strong:
I can open all the doors and tins
She could only paw at.

Dear pet crematorium
YOU DO NOT KNOW ME.
YOU DO NOT KNOW MY CAT.
All you know about my cat
Is her name.
All you know about me
Is that I used to have a cat.

Dear pet crematorium
You probably mean well
But you are out of your depth.
You just brought a Clintons card
To a knife fight.

If you'd known me, or my cat, you'd know
She was fierce
I remain fierce
And the soft underbelly of our bond
Was something earned.
Not everyone gets to pet its perfect fur.
Some bastards will get slashed for trying.

Our bond was built in claws, swearing
Grudging mutual respect, and time.
She was a crabby, traumatised old lady
I was a young idiot
Who didn't know what I'd taken on.

Across four years, four homes,
And fourteen different housemates
She unfurled in my care
I grew up in hers.

We curled up asleep against each other
– against the world –
Every night.

Dear pet crematorium
Thanks for the suggestion
But I do not need to look for my cat
'In the first ray of sunshine'
Or 'in the smile on a baby'
Or 'in the clear cool water on a quiet pond'.

Dear pet crematorium
Why the fuck would my cat
Be in a pond?!

Dear pet crematorium
Let's all stick to our real jobs:
My cat was not a poet.
I am no one's mum.
You are not spirit mediums.

Dear pet crematorium
Do not put words in my dead cat's mouth.
I paid you to burn her remains
Not do a ventriloquist routine
With her memory.

Dear pet crematorium
My gorgeous monster is not here
To vomit anymore
But I may do it for her.

NECROKITTY EPILOGUE

This house move I won't worry about you
Crying in the van.
You won't miss it
But I cried
Throwing out your basket.

ESTEEM

'COULD I HAVE SOME OF THAT TOO?'

Easter 2005.
I remember when because at the end
Of our long weekend
We wrote the date in spent roaches
Photographed it in fits of giggles
Amazed at how many we'd smoked.
We even had enough spare
To put a dotted line around the words
Easter 2005.
We were free, we were alive
We were lightweights.
Passing spliffs, crisps, cans and sweets.

'Oh, could I have some of that too?'

We are old enough to cook for ourselves
And young enough that this is a novelty.
We are hyper, fuelled by cider, M&Ms, herbs and spices.
I'm the oldest by a year, so my ID somehow snuck
A trolley full of booze
Past disapproving checkout clerks.
The Easter holiday unrolls before us
In rolling Devon hills
And a holiday home we were somehow allowed in.

'Oh, could I have some of that too?'

Meet the person I want to talk about.
Let's call her Jo, because Jo isn't her name.
I don't know her that well, but the ten of us are friends;
We must be if we're all here.
Everything we have is pooled.
We are so abundant in stuff, there aren't any rules:
Passing to the left took too long
So we pass one each way, and maybe a wildcard third
While Rosie rolls a fourth
Sitting in the long grass in the sunshine.

'Oh, could I have some of that too?'

Jo doesn't seem to know she's one of us.
Jo doesn't seem to know she's allowed.
Every time we pass something around
– and everything is always passed around –
Jo doesn't seem to know
That it's already coming her way.
Jo's refrain over these few days is a timid

'Oh, could I have some of that too?'

Initially, we said, 'Sure! Of course!'
But three days in and it's wearing thin.
She has been told she's welcome so many times
But still, every instance needs assurance
That she can have: a jelly baby, a puff, some dinner.
Sometimes it makes you feel rushed:
'Yes, everyone gets some pasta, just let me dish it out.'
Sometimes it makes you feel bad
That nothing you say can put her at ease
But after four days of checking if she is allowed
Four days of needing assurance
It's becoming self-fulfilling.

'Oh, could I have some of that too?'

This checking 'am I included, too?'
Creates a gap.
I never saw her as not part of the crowd
Until she kept letting us know
She felt like an interloper.

'Oh, could I have some of that too?'

It's five days in and I've lost patience.
Breaking down her disbelief
Is manual labour I can't be bothered with.
I don't care enough to coax this frightened animal
Out of her burrow
Every time we pass some Pringles.

We are all entitled to some Haribo
A look at that funny text, a toke.
Of course you can have a toke! Are you joking?
It's going around in a circle – that's how it works!
The food is here, the booze is here, we are all sharing it all around.
We are all welcome to it.
If that's not enough for you, then just – just –

I'm not proud of myself.
But this verbal tic is taking its toll.
Too many pleases put you down
Down one rung
Down one rank.
Now when I hear

'Oh, could I have some of that too?'

I want to say no.
I hear others do it too:
The 'yeah, sure'
Has become 'in a minute'
The 'of course you can'
Has become 'we'll see how much we've got left.'

'Oh, could I have some of that too?'

2005 was a while ago.
We were free, we were alive
We were lightweights.
I can remember the holiday home
But not everyone's name
And life has knocked me on my arse
Numerous times since then.
These days, when things are going my way
Often the first thing I feel is disbelief:
I double-check, triple-check

'Oh, could I have some of that too?'

Jo, I think of you more often than I want to admit
And Jo, I'm sorry.
I remember you clearly
Not just because I know I was a bit of a dick.

These days I often find myself waiting
For someone else to welcome me
Waiting for some big shiny sign to say I am allowed
To things it's no one else's call to say.

And I think back to you, and Easter
And all those endless puffs of tea
And wonder how often I've put up my own walls
Driven things away with my disbelief:
– of course the hot guy was just being friendly
– of course that promoter was just being polite
– of course my friend actually didn't mean it when they said
'Come crash with me in Spain any time
And I'm not just saying that, I really mean it.'

Jo, you weren't just some friend of a friend on a long weekend.
I remember you clearly now
Because I've always known your timid voice.
I knew it long before I met you.
I can try to put this in the past, call it Exhibit A
Label this specimen with the date Easter 2005 and your name
But sometimes, when things are going my way
Or when people I look up to treat me as an equal
Often all I can think is:
'Are you sure?'
'This must be some mistake.'
'I'm trespassing at this pub table.'

And all I need is a little reassurance
Someone to hold my hand and guide it
Teach it to reach out and accept what's already being offered
Instead of sitting on sidelines
Waiting, wondering, worrying whether:

'Oh, could I have some of that too?'

TAUT

You with the dark eyes
The electric smile
And the relationship:
Your attention pulled me taut.
I walked your compliments like a tightrope
Wobbled between aloof and over-eager
Dismounted with a bow
Cheek-kiss goodbye
Walked home alone, unsure of the show
All sickly yearning and heartstring regret.

RETURNING THESE DEMONS

I am returning these demons
You tried to give me
Palmed off as mine all along.
They have been fed and watered
Wearied on long walks
Hyped up on candyfloss and fairground rides.
They squealed and squabbled
The whole ride back.
But they were never mine.
Nice try.
Their holiday is over:
Back to you.
The little red one needs a nap.
Good luck.

PERMISSION

This is for the women who don't ask permission
To be themselves.
This is for the women who are done
With working on their contentment
And started working on their lot.

This is for the women whose posture says
'Fuck you, punk. I got it covered.'
This is for the women who've come too damn far
To waste time worrying whether you approve.
This is for the women who wear what they want
Swear how they want
Drink and fuck and love and fight
And wring every ounce like it's only their business –
Because it is.
And they've realised.

This is for the girl in class who's done with playing dumb.
Yes, she knows the answer –
Yes, no one else has put their hand up for the last ten minutes –
Yes, the teacher is looking past her raised hand asking
'Does anyone know the answer?
Anyone… else?'
But she'll be damned if she'll hide her own light.

This is for the gay bar barmaids who know their regulars
Inside and out
And wear those memories proud:
Like diamonds.
This is for the sweet little old lady
With the dirtiest laugh in the nursing home.
This is for my godmother Sara:
Terminal, regal, naughty
And 'educating' her doctors about the munchies.

This is for the liberated women
Who worked past violence and ridicule
To ensure that their daughters
Never needed to be liberated.

This is for the tough old birds
And the earnest youngsters
Who know that life is too personal, too precious
Too goddamn important
To let the magazines take a slice.

This is for the women who've stopped counting calories
And started counting stars.

This is for Dorothy Parker's forked tongue
Patti Smith's horses
Boudicca's chariots
And Rosa Parks' tired feet.

This is for the women we could be, can be, will be
Just as soon as we stop
      Asking permission
         To be.

SNAKESKIN

Years after I realised
'Let's stay friends'
Was a promise only worth keeping
For people worth keeping
After the unfriend, the block
The Darth Vader ringtone
So I know when it's bad news calling
She asks why I have a problem with her.

I want to give her a laundry list
Say, 'Drop a beat
And I'll spit you my three-hour freestyle
On the ways you are a sociopath'
But these days
I know a trap when I see one.

So I say
'Snakeskin.'

Your idea of who I am
Is a pale outline
Which hasn't fit for years.
You're grasping at a ghost;
I have grown, split my skin and moved on
Countless times since then.

I know you think you know
Where the sore spots are
But I have cast off every inch of skin
You ever touched
Shed that shadow and slithered on
Not because of you –
It's just what we do.

So hold tight
To the memories;
You're only holding snakeskin.

Sure, you charmed me once
Held me mesmerised
While I swallowed your stories whole
But I'm not spineless;
I'm flexible.
I can always wriggle free.
And I'm never going back in a basket.
I don't hide under rocks; I bask.

When we met, change was overdue.
I was faded, constricted
With cloudy eyes and skin that barely fit
So I split and discarded it
Kept winding my way
Flickering my tongue
My scales shining that deep gloss
That was always there
Beneath.

I've just remembered you're afraid of snakes
And that only makes it better
When I say:

My old skin holds the shape
Of the smaller me
The one that you once knew.
So hold as tight as you like
To my shadow's tail;

You're only holding snakeskin.

THE KIND OF PERFECT I READ AS THREAT

She looks the kind of perfect I read as 'threat':
Makeup airbrush-perfect over killer cheekbones
Conventionally drop-dead gorgeous
Skintight dress, skin glowing
Siren.

Years of feminist theory
Cannot silence the feral, playground voice:
'She will pick on you.'
'Run away now.'
But in this cramped pub toilet
I need to get to the sink.

I smile an ingratiating 'excuse me'.
She switches mirrors
To repaint perfect lipstick on bee-stung lips.
I try not to steal glances
In the mirror facing me.

I 'sorry, excuse me' to the hand dryer
As my high school bathrooms close in around me
Like a time machine.
If I remember my place, bow my head
She'll probably leave me be.

But this place is so small.
I 'sorry, excuse me' again to the door
And she asks me
'Do I look OK?'

The time machine jerks to a halt.

For the first time I look up properly
Mumble a 'Yeah. Yeah, you do.'
And this perfect-looking girl
Exhales relief.

'OK… yeah, thanks.'
Smiles.
Looks grateful.
Looks at the floor.

And the time machine blows out
Spinning tiles in all directions.

BRAIN WEEDING

I am weeding the ground of my mind
Picking through the thoughts that grow
Deciding which I want to keep
Digging others out at the root.

Some are fine but there isn't space.
Some will not survive my soil.
Some scattered seeds I never noticed
Until they sprouted seasons later.

Some pull out cleanly
Others put up a fight:
Rhizomes of anxiety, self-sabotage
Stretch subterranean across my landscape
Shooting new spears through the surface
When I thought I'd got them all.

But this newly-bare earth is not empty
This blank space will not stay blank:
It is a tidy room
A new notebook
Fertile ground
In which to plant
For next season.

SELF-TRANSCENDENCE
AND
SELF-ACTUALISATION

LEVEL

I like the way it flirts as you say it:
Tongue tip to the roof of your mouth
Bite lip
Tongue tip back and smile:
Level.

I like a level playing field
Will dig this land to make it happen.
I aspire to its calm, even keel:
Level.

I like that it holds a mirror
Within itself:
L-e-v-e-L
Eve in brackets.

To level with you
I love how it contains levels:
Levelling up as I grow
Levellers, Diggers, Quakers, all my left-wing history
Calm seas, lover-gentle, the quality of equality

And it flirts as you say it:
Tongue tip to the roof of your mouth
Bite lip
Tongue tip back and smile.

BOTTLE GARDEN

I was aiming for the happily ever after
Of a bottle garden
Add the right ingredients and watch it go:
Simple, cycled, perpetual.

But my life is not sealed
Not simple
Not cycled.

Some plants withered whether I watered them or not
Some plants succumbed to spiteful aphid attack
Some grew well but my enthusiasm didn't
And others
Grow stronger, quicker, more beautiful than I knew possible
Sprout flowers and seeds I never expected
Until their stretching roots tangle
Take up every inch of room they are allowed.

My halfway to happily ever after
Needs repotting
Rethinking
And more than a windowsill
To grow on.

AUTUMN MOM

Autumn was always my favourite season
But it doesn't look like autumn from here.

Sixty brought demob happy
Before it began
The thought kicking around her mind
Like a truanting kid:
'I don't *have* to be here.'

She bought herself an iPad
With the leaving gift vouchers
And a better banjo.
The summer holidays ended
The school bell rang
The school gates closed
With her outside
In the garden
Second cup of coffee
Cat
Colour supplement.

Autumn was always my favourite season
But it doesn't look like autumn from here.

Sometimes she meets me at work.
We go for lunch where the city boys eat sushi.
She still doesn't let me pay
Shows photos on the iPad
Talks two lots of volunteering
Museums and walks
Brings home-grown grapes and plums
Jars of home-made jam

Yoga, Pilates, swimming
Well slept for the first time in thirty-two years
Mortgage paid off
Garden in bloom

Gigs a few times a month
With her band
With their CD.

Autumn was always my favourite season
But it doesn't look like autumn from here
Unless we mean
Bringing in the harvest.

BUTTERFLIES

We were searching for silver, we were greedy for gold
Miss said it was just a flint rock but we wouldn't be told
'Cause we'd found a fossilised T-rex claw
And Mariko was a dragon and the world was so much more
Than rocks and lunchboxes and broken things
We had alchemy and treasure and butterfly wings.

Today I lost my earring in the swimming pool
Felt around and found: only one silver stud.
Damnit, I liked them, wore them all the time
Just little silver dots with a rhinestone shine.

My grown-up lengths gave way
To searching, scavenging along the pool floor.
I'd duck-dive down and trawl the tiles
Looking for those two tiny pieces of silver.

And every time I duck-dived down
I felt myself diving deeper
Back through time, to when
– back then –
Every Saturday morning
Swimming lesson over, I'd go
– tip-toe –
To the grown-up pool
And with a stout pair of lungs, and leaky goggles
I'd duck-dive down
Deep down to where the light dappled and danced
Fluttered on the pool floor.
I'd glide
– eagle-eyed –
Past plasters and broken hair grips
And I would go panning for gold.

I would catch golden butterfly backs
Carry them in the net of my swimming cap.
These tiny bits of lost earrings
– these butterfly backs with hard little wings –
Were my totemic treasure

Worth more than pocket money could quite measure.

I knew these things were useless, but I did this for years.
Back then I didn't even have pierced ears
'But look! I got one!
This is real gold. I'm holding gold!'

The same way we picked across gritted playgrounds
To pocket the highest-carat clear salt crystals
From the floor.

The same way me and my friend Simone
Spent lunchtimes huddled on our own
Picking shining droplets of solder
Off the pipes along the wall
And we'd hold these tiny orbs
Between thumb and forefinger:
'Look! I got one! This is silver!'

We were searching for silver, we were greedy for gold
Miss said it was just a flint rock but we wouldn't be told
'Cause we'd found a fossilised T-rex claw
And Mariko was a dragon and the world was so much more
Than asphalt and solder and broken things
We had alchemy and treasure and butterfly wings.

I stored all these gems in a tiny box
Next to the diary with the heart-shaped padlock
And under siege from my brother I'd create hiding places
   always seeking secret spaces –
To stash this dragon hoard in.

But now I'm a grown-up
So I'm 90% sure
The drain in the pool floor
Is not a trap door
For a shark.

And I own real silver (I don't much like gold)
And I know the prices of things 'cause I'm grown-up and old
But the value of things I'm never sure about
'Cause magic makes some room for doubt.

I'm trying not to be a hoarder. Try as I might
As my housemate begs me to bin all this useless shite
I can't stop believing that some of it's special.
Some of it's treasure.
Value is sometimes more than sense can measure.

And I'm still pissed I lost my earring
But to the treasure-hunting child who I hope finds it:
Yes, it is a real diamond
And real silver
– scrub that –
Platinum.
Keep it in a box full of conkers and sequins.
Look after it for me.
You are welcome.

BIRTHDAY BIRTHDAY CAKE

'Birthday! Birthday!'
'Cake?'
'Birthday! Birthday!'
'Cake?'

They have impressive blood alcohol levels
Little English
Huge grins
And a cake
The size of a Stetson hat.

A small section has been sliced and eaten
The rest is shop-bought pristine
And these two, drunk as lords
Dance through Slough's dark streets
Holding the cake aloft
Like a trophy.

I am shuffling, with colleagues
To the train
To the tube
To the bus
That will take me home.
We all cover too many miles
To have petrol left
For Fridays.

But these two guys
Are sugar-high gorgeous
Delighted
To have cake
And now
An audience.

'Birthday! Birthday!'
'Cake?'
'Birthday! Birthday!'
'Cake?'

'Whose birthday is it?' I ask.
Birthday Birthday points at Cake.
'Happy birthday!' I say.
Cake holds up one finger for 'wait'.
Birthday Birthday opens his bag
Pulls out, from packaging:
A paper plate, a plastic fork and a napkin.

'Oh, for me? Er… yeah, thanks!'
Birthday Birthday and Cake set about slicing a piece.
Cooperation takes concentration
But they manage
Giggling like schoolkids when they hand me
A plate, a fork and a slice.

I giggle a 'wow, thank you!'
Look back to my colleagues to offer…
They have frozen.
Holding back while Hannah
Talks to the weirdoes.

My new friends offer cake to them, too.
My workmates shrink back further.
'Hannah, we've got to get the train.'

I gesture 'got to go', say 'thank you' again
Say 'happy birthday' again.
Birthday Birthday hugs me.
Cake has his hands full with the cake
But nods goodbye with a grin
As wide as saloon doors.

I catch up with workmates
Have a forkful halfway to my mouth
When Matt from Design says
'You're going to eat it?!'
And Claire from Editorial says
'How do you know it's not poisoned?'

I eat the cake.
I do not die.
It is delicious.

FRESH WATER

There is a rib-knit scarf I bought for its shade of blue.
Its shiny Mylar strands that nestle in the wool
Make it sparkle like a stream in sunlight
But I never wear it.
Its shape is too long and thin
To keep the cold out.

Mid-clear-out I came across it:
Was about to throw it away 'til I realised
I could make it better
Break it down and rebuild.

I find my knitting needles and unpick one end
Cast straight on from the old scarf to the new.

Each row unravels its rivulets
Runs in rivers which I
Loop, knit and purl
Into the lake slowly pooling
Beneath the dam of my needles.

From skinny rib-knit I create
Wide, welcoming moss stitch
Knit one, purl one, flat and dappled
Soft and spongy, like the blankets my cat kneads
With outstretched, starfish paws.

My friend, not a knitter, comes over.
I knit as we talk over tea
The scarf growing, slow and steady
Beneath my fidgeting fingers.

She asks me to explain how I'm making this new thing.
I shrug, say it's just string.
She asks how I know if I'm doing it right.
I say it's just a building block
This wool can be worn, strung and structured
Dozens of different ways.

She looks at the old, unworn scarf
Unravelling and evolving into one I will love
Says, 'As someone with a fear of failure
It's really good to see it's not set in stone.'

I'd never seen it that way
Never saw my re-use as redemption
But she's not wrong.

Creativity gives second chances
Means you can make your own options
Teaches you to turn test papers to origami
Or confetti, spitwads, papier-mâché
Paperchain people or shadow puppets.

In truth, from one scarf to another
Isn't much at all
But this breaking it down and remaking
Is the difference
Between something so-so
And something special.

Creativity means knowing there are other options.
It's the difference between 'oh, that's a shame'
And 'oh, hell yeah'.
It isn't just win or lose, yes or no
There's always an 'also'.

Each row unravels its rivulets
Runs in rivers which I
Loop, knit and purl
Into the lake slowly pooling
Beneath the dam of my needles.

Each row unravels its rivulets
Runs in rivers which I
Loop, knit and purl
Into something larger
Something which keeps the cold out.

DARWIN'S WORMS

I'm fed up with perfection
Pedestals and pearls.
So little of the process survives the polish.

Finished products are more impressive, but less interesting
Than the ones with woodgrain showing
Springs hanging out.

Let me tell you about Charles Darwin and earthworms:
Though worms will respond to vibrations
(Raindrops or sneaky seagull feet)
Darwin wanted to know whether worms could hear.

He tested this by talking to the worms
…The worms did not respond.

Shouting at the worms
…The worms did not respond.

Clapping at the worms
…The worms did not respond.

Playing the piccolo to the worms
…The worms did not respond.

Playing the bassoon to the worms
…The worms did not respond.

Playing the drum to the worms
…The worms did not respond.

Playing the piano to the worms
…The worms did not respond.

Darwin concluded that worms are deaf.
But his book *Earthworms* remains
A leading text on the topic.

So little trial and error survives the edit
To be dignified by endpapers.

The people you admire from afar
Spotlit by status, sanded smooth by time
Looked a lot like madmen
In the moment.

Don't look up at the pedestal and despair
At your prospects of scaling those heights.
Peek around the back
To the winding paths that led there;
You will find passionate weirdos
Pursuing their thing
Playing the bassoon
To earthworms.

DRAWING DOWN THE MOON

The camera is close to magic but
The shutter needs your stillness
The space between your breaths
To work its miracle.

You never knew your heartbeat
Moved your fingertips
'Til now
Never meditated without meditating
'Til now.
Tripods help but still
The shutter needs your stillness.

The optical zoom can find
The brightest light in the sky
Brilliant blur then focus
Across 230,000 miles
Sketching landscape
Shade and crater
Across the moon you've always loved
But never seen so clearly as
Now.
You click to capture but you shifted.
The shutter needs your stillness.

It never draws a perfect circle.
Each night the slow shadow shows
Different craters, dappled grey seas
Each night conditions crisp or halo
Each photograph unfocussed in a different way
Each impressive and none perfect.
The shutter needs your stillness
And this, your nightly mandala
To seek
The space between your breaths
To try to draw down
A perfect circle.

ON SECOND THOUGHTS I'VE GOT COLD FEET, I MEAN JESUS ANYONE COULD READ THIS

Ctrl + Z
Everything I said.

ACKNOWLEDGEMENTS

I'll be forever grateful to Mr Savage and Miss Cottrell, my best ever English teachers, for their early encouragement. Endless gratitude also to Megan Bettinson – my personal cheerleader since Sixth Form.

Heartfelt and huggy thanks to all the individuals, groups, nights and networks who've been invaluable for support, inspiration, encouragement and sometimes unflinching feedback. Especially Anna Kahn, Catalina Ferro, Cat Brogan, Chris Farnell, Fay Roberts, Gemma Scott, Hannah Morgan, Jake Wild-Hall, Karen Grace, Matt MacDonald, Niall Spooner-Harvey, Raphael Kabo, Maddie Godfrey and the 30/30 Group, Apples and Snakes, Boomerang Club, the Creative Union of Nuanced Thinkers & Scribblers (C.U.N.T.S), Forget What You Heard About Spoken Word, Hammer & Tongue, Jawdance, the London Poetry and Recreation Society Members Club for Girls, LossLit, Other Voices, PBH Free Fringe, the Spirit of the Rainbow Heron Trust, the Rumour Cubes, the Whippersnapper Press crew and Write Club Norwich. Thanks also to Sophia Blackwell and Tim Clare for existing.

To everyone who's let me overshare our shared stories – you know who you are. Thank you.

Some of these poems have appeared previously in other publications, including my two previous collections *Alchemy Treasure* and *Butterfly Wings*, published by Allographic Press, and *Sign My Citalopram*, published by the Spirit of the Rainbow Heron. 'This Is Your Twenties', 'No Little Words' and 'Butterflies' have appeared in various Poetry Rivals anthologies. 'Job Centre' appeared in the Morning Star, 'A Dude in an East London Pub' appeared in Rising magazine, 'Necrokitty Comic Sans' and 'Snakeskin' both appeared in the London Spoken Word Anthology. 'I Called You Captain' appears as a track on Before Victoria's album *The Sad Machines*.